A WINE
LOVER'S
DIARY

WINE LOVER _Patricia Banziger_

DIARY KEPT BETWEEN _Dec. 25/2000_ AND _____

A WINE
LOVER'S
DIARY

FIREFLY BOOKS

A FIREFLY BOOK

Published by Firefly Books Ltd., 1999

First Printing

A Wine Lover's Diary
ISBN 1-55209-369-7

Published in Canada in 1999 by Firefly Books Ltd.,
3680 Victoria Park Avenue, Willowdale, Ontario, Canada M2H 3K1

Published in the United States in 1999 by Firefly Books (U.S.) Inc.
P.O. Box 1338, Ellicott Station, Buffalo, New York 14205

Conceived and edited by Shelagh Wallace and Jock Sutherland
Illustrated and designed by Scott McKowen

Printed in Canada

Quotations from *In Praise of Wine: An Offering of Hearty Toasts, Quotations,
Witticisms, Proverbs, and Poetry throughout History* by Joni McNutt reprinted
by permission of Capra Press.

Quotations from *Travels with my Corkscrew: Memoirs of a Wine Lover* by
Tony Aspler reprinted by permission of McGraw-Hill Ryerson Limited.

Quotation from *Seven Gothic Tales* by Isak Dinesen reprinted by permission
of Random House, Inc.

With grateful thanks to Jock Sutherland, Colleen Cowman, Robert Cluett,
Glen Muir and Sandra Marynissen of Marynissen Winery, James Morris
of Rundles Restaruant, Billy Munnelly of Best Bottles, Judy Scott and
Rob Sproat.

*The Publisher acknowledges the financial support of the Government of Canada
through the Book Publishing Industry Development Program for its publishing
activities.*

Acknowledgements
We wish to thank those publishers who have given their permission
to reproduce excerpts from works still in copyright. If anyone has been
unintentionally omitted, we offer our apologies and ask that you notify
the publisher so you may be included in future editions.

TABLE OF CONTENTS

The discovery of wine is of greater moment than the discovery of a constellation. The universe is too full of stars.

ANTHELME BRILLAT-SAVARIN

Wine sloweth age, it strengtheneth youth, it helpeth digestion, it abandoneth melancholie, it relisheth the heart, it lighteneth the mind, it quickeneth the spirits, it keepeth and preserveth the head from whirling, the eyes from dazzling, the tongue from lisping, the mouth from snaffling, the teeth from chattering, and the throat from rattling; it keepeth the stomach from wambling, the heart from swelling, the hands from shivering, the sinews from shrinking, the veins from crumbling, the bones from aching, and the marrow from soaking.

13TH CENTURY ANONYMOUS

THE WINE LIST

WINE NAME

DESCRIPTION

RECOMMENDED BY

PRICE / VENDOR

WINE NAME

DESCRIPTION

RECOMMENDED BY

PRICE / VENDOR

WINE NAME

DESCRIPTION

RECOMMENDED BY

PRICE / VENDOR

WINE NAME

DESCRIPTION

RECOMMENDED BY

PRICE / VENDOR

WINE NAME

DESCRIPTION

RECOMMENDED BY

PRICE / VENDOR

WINE NAME

DESCRIPTION

RECOMMENDED BY

PRICE / VENDOR

WINE NAME

DESCRIPTION

RECOMMENDED BY

PRICE / VENDOR

WINE NAME

DESCRIPTION

RECOMMENDED BY

PRICE / VENDOR

WINE NAME

DESCRIPTION

RECOMMENDED BY

PRICE / VENDOR

 *ood wine gladdens the eye, cleans the teeth, and heals the stomach.*

SPANISH PROVERB

WINE NAME

DESCRIPTION

RECOMMENDED BY

PRICE / VENDOR

WINE NAME

DESCRIPTION

RECOMMENDED BY

PRICE / VENDOR

WINE NAME

DESCRIPTION

RECOMMENDED BY

PRICE / VENDOR

WINE NAME

DESCRIPTION

RECOMMENDED BY

PRICE / VENDOR

WINE NAME

DESCRIPTION

RECOMMENDED BY

PRICE / VENDOR

WINE NAME

DESCRIPTION

RECOMMENDED BY

PRICE / VENDOR

WINE NAME

DESCRIPTION

RECOMMENDED BY

PRICE / VENDOR

WINE NAME

DESCRIPTION

RECOMMENDED BY

PRICE / VENDOR

WINE NAME

DESCRIPTION

RECOMMENDED BY

PRICE / VENDOR

WINE NAME

DESCRIPTION

RECOMMENDED BY

PRICE / VENDOR

WINE NAME

DESCRIPTION

RECOMMENDED BY

PRICE / VENDOR

WINE NAME

DESCRIPTION

RECOMMENDED BY

PRICE / VENDOR

WINE NAME

DESCRIPTION

RECOMMENDED BY

PRICE / VENDOR

f wine is taken in the right measure it suits every age, every time and every region. It is becoming to the old because it opposes their dryness. To the young it is a food, because the nature of wine is the same as that of young people...it increases their natural heat.

ARNALDUS: *LIBER DE VINIS*, GREEK PHYSICIAN (C.1235-1311)

WINE NAME

DESCRIPTION

RECOMMENDED BY

PRICE / VENDOR

WINE NAME

DESCRIPTION

RECOMMENDED BY

PRICE / VENDOR

WINE NAME

DESCRIPTION

RECOMMENDED BY

PRICE / VENDOR

WINE NAME

DESCRIPTION

RECOMMENDED BY

PRICE / VENDOR

WINE NAME

DESCRIPTION

RECOMMENDED BY

PRICE / VENDOR

WINE NAME

DESCRIPTION

RECOMMENDED BY

PRICE / VENDOR

WINE NAME

DESCRIPTION

RECOMMENDED BY

PRICE / VENDOR

WINE NAME

DESCRIPTION

RECOMMENDED BY

PRICE / VENDOR

ine has the property of heating the parts of the body inside when it is drunk and of cooling them when poured on the outside.

PLINY THE ELDER

WINE NAME

DESCRIPTION

RECOMMENDED BY

PRICE / VENDOR

WINE NAME

DESCRIPTION

RECOMMENDED BY

PRICE / VENDOR

WINE NAME

DESCRIPTION

RECOMMENDED BY

PRICE / VENDOR

WINE NAME

DESCRIPTION

RECOMMENDED BY

PRICE / VENDOR

WINE NAME

DESCRIPTION

RECOMMENDED BY

PRICE / VENDOR

THE WINE LIST – WINES TO TRY

WINE NAME

DESCRIPTION

RECOMMENDED BY

PRICE / VENDOR

WINE NAME

DESCRIPTION

RECOMMENDED BY

PRICE / VENDOR

WINE NAME

DESCRIPTION

RECOMMENDED BY

PRICE / VENDOR

WINE NAME

DESCRIPTION

RECOMMENDED BY

PRICE / VENDOR

 *ine is at the head of all medicines; where wine is lacking, drugs are necessary.*

BABYLONIAN TALMUD

WINE NAME

DESCRIPTION

RECOMMENDED BY

PRICE / VENDOR

WINE NAME

DESCRIPTION

RECOMMENDED BY

PRICE / VENDOR

WINE NAME

DESCRIPTION

RECOMMENDED BY

PRICE / VENDOR

WINE NAME

DESCRIPTION

RECOMMENDED BY

PRICE / VENDOR

WINE NAME

DESCRIPTION

RECOMMENDED BY

PRICE / VENDOR

If with water you fill up your glasses, You'll never write anything wise; For wine is the horse of Parnassus, Which hurries a bard to the skies.

THOMAS MOORE: *ANACREONTIC*

THE WINE
RECORD

WINE NAME OYSTER BAY [NEW ZEALAND · MARLBOROUGH

OCCASION

PRICE / VENDOR

DESCRIPTION SAV BLANC

REVIEW

WINE NAME GOLDRIDGE ESTATE - [MARLBOROUGH NZ]

OCCASION

PRICE / VENDOR $22

DESCRIPTION SAV BLANC (Gooseberry passionfruit - crisp ligh

REVIEW

WINE NAME WARRENMANG

OCCASION

PRICE / VENDOR $55

DESCRIPTION SHIRAZ (SPICE, PLUM, RIBENA, VANILIN OAK · 50

REVIEW GOOD

WINE NAME THE SHOW [NAPA VALLEY]

OCCASION

PRICE / VENDOR $18.00

DESCRIPTION CAB SAV

REVIEW

WINE NAME _THE SHOW_

OCCASION

PRICE / VENDOR _$18.00_

DESCRIPTION _MELBEL_

REVIEW _AMAZING_

WINE NAME

OCCASION

PRICE / VENDOR

DESCRIPTION

REVIEW

WINE NAME

OCCASION

PRICE / VENDOR

DESCRIPTION

REVIEW

ine is a magician, for it loosens the tongue and liberates good stories.

HOMER

WINE NAME

OCCASION

PRICE / VENDOR

DESCRIPTION

REVIEW

WINE NAME

OCCASION

PRICE / VENDOR

DESCRIPTION

REVIEW

WINE NAME

OCCASION

PRICE / VENDOR

DESCRIPTION

REVIEW

 ine in moderation – not in excess, for that makes men ugly – has a thousand pleasant influences. It brightens the eye, improves the voice, imparts a new vivacity to one's thoughts and conversation.

CHARLES DICKENS: *BARNABY RUDGE*

WINE NAME

OCCASION

PRICE / VENDOR

DESCRIPTION

REVIEW

WINE NAME

OCCASION

PRICE / VENDOR

DESCRIPTION

REVIEW

WINE NAME

OCCASION

PRICE / VENDOR

DESCRIPTION

REVIEW

WINE NAME

OCCASION

PRICE / VENDOR

DESCRIPTION

REVIEW

WINE NAME

OCCASION

PRICE / VENDOR

DESCRIPTION

REVIEW

WINE NAME

OCCASION

PRICE / VENDOR

DESCRIPTION

REVIEW

WINE NAME

OCCASION

PRICE / VENDOR

DESCRIPTION

REVIEW

WINE NAME

OCCASION

PRICE / VENDOR

DESCRIPTION

REVIEW

WINE NAME

OCCASION

PRICE / VENDOR

DESCRIPTION

REVIEW

WINE NAME

OCCASION

PRICE / VENDOR

DESCRIPTION

REVIEW

WINE NAME

OCCASION

PRICE / VENDOR

DESCRIPTION

REVIEW

WINE NAME

OCCASION

PRICE / VENDOR

DESCRIPTION

REVIEW

WINE NAME

OCCASION

PRICE / VENDOR

DESCRIPTION

REVIEW

WINE NAME

OCCASION

PRICE / VENDOR

DESCRIPTION

REVIEW

WINE NAME

OCCASION

PRICE / VENDOR

DESCRIPTION

REVIEW

WINE NAME

OCCASION

PRICE / VENDOR

DESCRIPTION

REVIEW

WINE NAME

OCCASION

PRICE / VENDOR

DESCRIPTION

REVIEW

WINE NAME

OCCASION

PRICE / VENDOR

DESCRIPTION

REVIEW

WINE NAME

OCCASION

PRICE / VENDOR

DESCRIPTION

REVIEW

man will be eloquent if you give him good wine.

RALPH WALDO EMERSON

29

WINE NAME

OCCASION

PRICE / VENDOR

DESCRIPTION

REVIEW

WINE NAME

OCCASION

PRICE / VENDOR

DESCRIPTION

REVIEW

WINE NAME

OCCASION

PRICE / VENDOR

DESCRIPTION

REVIEW

WINE NAME

OCCASION

PRICE / VENDOR

DESCRIPTION

REVIEW

WINE NAME

OCCASION

PRICE / VENDOR

DESCRIPTION

REVIEW

WINE NAME

OCCASION

PRICE / VENDOR

DESCRIPTION

REVIEW

WINE NAME

OCCASION

PRICE / VENDOR

DESCRIPTION

REVIEW

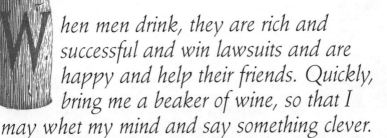

When men drink, they are rich and successful and win lawsuits and are happy and help their friends. Quickly, bring me a beaker of wine, so that I may whet my mind and say something clever.

ARISTOPHANES: *THE KNIGHTS*

WINE NAME

OCCASION

PRICE / VENDOR

DESCRIPTION

REVIEW

WINE NAME

OCCASION

PRICE / VENDOR

DESCRIPTION

REVIEW

WINE NAME

OCCASION

PRICE / VENDOR

DESCRIPTION

REVIEW

There is no harm in doing one's thinking and writing while slightly drunk, and then revising one's work in cold blood. The stimulus of wine is favorable to the play of invention, and to fluency of expression.

G.C. LICHTENBERG, GERMAN PHYSICIST AND SATIRIST (1742-99)

WINE NAME

OCCASION

PRICE / VENDOR

DESCRIPTION

REVIEW

WINE NAME

OCCASION

PRICE / VENDOR

DESCRIPTION

REVIEW

WINE NAME

OCCASION

PRICE / VENDOR

DESCRIPTION

REVIEW

WINE NAME

OCCASION

PRICE / VENDOR

DESCRIPTION

REVIEW

WINE NAME

OCCASION

PRICE / VENDOR

DESCRIPTION

REVIEW

WINE NAME

OCCASION

PRICE / VENDOR

DESCRIPTION

REVIEW

WINE NAME

OCCASION

PRICE / VENDOR

DESCRIPTION

REVIEW

WINE NAME

OCCASION

PRICE / VENDOR

DESCRIPTION

REVIEW

WINE NAME

OCCASION

PRICE / VENDOR

DESCRIPTION

REVIEW

WINE NAME

OCCASION

PRICE / VENDOR

DESCRIPTION

REVIEW

WINE NAME

OCCASION

PRICE / VENDOR

DESCRIPTION

REVIEW

WINE NAME

OCCASION

PRICE / VENDOR

DESCRIPTION

REVIEW

WINE NAME

OCCASION

PRICE / VENDOR

DESCRIPTION

REVIEW

WINE NAME

OCCASION

PRICE / VENDOR

DESCRIPTION

REVIEW

WINE NAME

OCCASION

PRICE / VENDOR

DESCRIPTION

REVIEW

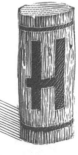

ow great a thing is a single cup of wine! For it makes us tell the story of our whole lives.

PO CHU-I, CHINESE POET (772-846)

WINE NAME

OCCASION

PRICE / VENDOR

DESCRIPTION

REVIEW

WINE NAME

OCCASION

PRICE / VENDOR

DESCRIPTION

REVIEW

WINE NAME

OCCASION

PRICE / VENDOR

DESCRIPTION

REVIEW

WINE NAME

OCCASION

PRICE / VENDOR

DESCRIPTION

REVIEW

WINE NAME

OCCASION

PRICE / VENDOR

DESCRIPTION

REVIEW

WINE NAME

OCCASION

PRICE / VENDOR

DESCRIPTION

REVIEW

WINE NAME

OCCASION

PRICE / VENDOR

DESCRIPTION

REVIEW

WINE NAME

OCCASION

PRICE / VENDOR

DESCRIPTION

REVIEW

WINE NAME

OCCASION

PRICE / VENDOR

DESCRIPTION

REVIEW

WINE NAME

OCCASION

PRICE / VENDOR

DESCRIPTION

REVIEW

ine has been to me a firm friend and a wise counsellor. Often, wine has shown me matters in their true perspective, and has, as though by the touch of a magic wand, reduced great disasters to small inconveniences. Wine has lit up for me the pages of literature, and revealed romance lurking in the commonplace.

ALFRED DUFF COOPER, BRITISH STATESMAN AND AUTHOR (1890-1954)

WINE NAME

OCCASION

PRICE / VENDOR

DESCRIPTION

REVIEW

WINE NAME

OCCASION

PRICE / VENDOR

DESCRIPTION

REVIEW

WINE NAME

OCCASION

PRICE / VENDOR

DESCRIPTION

REVIEW

WINE NAME

OCCASION

PRICE / VENDOR

DESCRIPTION

REVIEW

WINE NAME

OCCASION

PRICE / VENDOR

DESCRIPTION

REVIEW

WINE NAME

OCCASION

PRICE / VENDOR

DESCRIPTION

REVIEW

WINE NAME

OCCASION

PRICE / VENDOR

DESCRIPTION

REVIEW

ine will make a man intelligent.

BABYLONIAN TALMUD: *JOMA*

ankind possesses two supreme blessings. First of these is the goddess Demeter, or Earth...It was she who gave to man his nourishment of grain. But after her there came the son of Semele, who matched her present by inventing liquid wine as his gift to man. For filled with that good gift, suffering mankind forgets its grief; from it comes sleep; with it oblivion of the troubles of the day. There is no other medicine for misery.

EURIPIDES: *THE BACCHAE*

THE WINE CELLAR

WINE NAME

VINTAGE SPECIFICS

PRICE / VENDOR

RECOMMENDED BY

OCCASION / GIFT FOR

WINE NAME

VINTAGE SPECIFICS

PRICE / VENDOR

RECOMMENDED BY

OCCASION / GIFT FOR

WINE NAME

VINTAGE SPECIFICS

PRICE / VENDOR

RECOMMENDED BY

OCCASION / GIFT FOR

*od made only water,
but man made wine.*

VICTOR HUGO (1802-1885)

WINE NAME

VINTAGE SPECIFICS

PRICE / VENDOR

RECOMMENDED BY

OCCASION / GIFT FOR

WINE NAME

VINTAGE SPECIFICS

PRICE / VENDOR

RECOMMENDED BY

OCCASION / GIFT FOR

WINE NAME

VINTAGE SPECIFICS

PRICE / VENDOR

RECOMMENDED BY

OCCASION / GIFT FOR

WINE NAME

VINTAGE SPECIFICS

PRICE / VENDOR

RECOMMENDED BY

OCCASION / GIFT FOR

WINE NAME

VINTAGE SPECIFICS

PRICE / VENDOR

RECOMMENDED BY

OCCASION / GIFT FOR

WINE NAME

VINTAGE SPECIFICS

PRICE / VENDOR

RECOMMENDED BY

OCCASION / GIFT FOR

WINE NAME

VINTAGE SPECIFICS

PRICE / VENDOR

RECOMMENDED BY

OCCASION / GIFT FOR

WINE NAME

VINTAGE SPECIFICS

PRICE / VENDOR

RECOMMENDED BY

OCCASION / GIFT FOR

WINE NAME

VINTAGE SPECIFICS

PRICE / VENDOR

RECOMMENDED BY

OCCASION / GIFT FOR

WINE NAME

VINTAGE SPECIFICS

PRICE / VENDOR

RECOMMENDED BY

OCCASION / GIFT FOR

WINE NAME

VINTAGE SPECIFICS

PRICE / VENDOR

RECOMMENDED BY

OCCASION / GIFT FOR

hat is man, when you come to think upon him, but a minutely set, ingenious machine for turning, with infinite artfulness, the red wine of Shiraz into urine?

ISAK DINESEN: *SEVEN GOTHIC TALES*

THE WINE CELLAR – WINES TO BUY

WINE NAME

VINTAGE SPECIFICS

PRICE / VENDOR

RECOMMENDED BY

OCCASION / GIFT FOR

WINE NAME

VINTAGE SPECIFICS

PRICE / VENDOR

RECOMMENDED BY

OCCASION / GIFT FOR

WINE NAME

VINTAGE SPECIFICS

PRICE / VENDOR

RECOMMENDED BY

OCCASION / GIFT FOR

 *ood wine makes good blood,
good blood causeth good humours,
good humours causeth good thoughts,
good thoughts bring forth good works,
good works carry a man to Heaven; ergo
good wine carrieth a man to Heaven.*

JAMES HOWELL, ENGLISH AUTHOR (C.1594-1666)

WINE NAME

VINTAGE SPECIFICS

PRICE / VENDOR

RECOMMENDED BY

OCCASION / GIFT FOR

WINE NAME

VINTAGE SPECIFICS

PRICE / VENDOR

RECOMMENDED BY

OCCASION / GIFT FOR

WINE NAME

VINTAGE SPECIFICS

PRICE / VENDOR

RECOMMENDED BY

OCCASION / GIFT FOR

WINE NAME

VINTAGE SPECIFICS

PRICE / VENDOR

RECOMMENDED BY

OCCASION / GIFT FOR

WINE NAME

VINTAGE SPECIFICS

PRICE / VENDOR

RECOMMENDED BY

OCCASION / GIFT FOR

WINE NAME

VINTAGE SPECIFICS

PRICE / VENDOR

RECOMMENDED BY

OCCASION / GIFT FOR

WINE NAME

VINTAGE SPECIFICS

PRICE / VENDOR

RECOMMENDED BY

OCCASION / GIFT FOR

ever think of giving perfumes or wines to your heir. Let him have your money, but give these to yourself. MARTIAL: *EPIGRAMS*

WINE NAME

VINTAGE SPECIFICS

PRICE / VENDOR

RECOMMENDED BY

OCCASION / GIFT FOR

WINE NAME

VINTAGE SPECIFICS

PRICE / VENDOR

RECOMMENDED BY

OCCASION / GIFT FOR

WINE NAME

VINTAGE SPECIFICS

PRICE / VENDOR

RECOMMENDED BY

OCCASION / GIFT FOR

WINE NAME

VINTAGE SPECIFICS

PRICE / VENDOR

RECOMMENDED BY

OCCASION / GIFT FOR

WINE NAME

VINTAGE SPECIFICS

PRICE / VENDOR

RECOMMENDED BY

OCCASION / GIFT FOR

WINE NAME

VINTAGE SPECIFICS

PRICE / VENDOR

RECOMMENDED BY

OCCASION / GIFT FOR

WINE NAME

VINTAGE SPECIFICS

PRICE / VENDOR

RECOMMENDED BY

OCCASION / GIFT FOR

WINE NAME

VINTAGE SPECIFICS

PRICE / VENDOR

RECOMMENDED BY

OCCASION / GIFT FOR

WINE NAME

VINTAGE SPECIFICS

PRICE / VENDOR

RECOMMENDED BY

OCCASION / GIFT FOR

WINE NAME

VINTAGE SPECIFICS

PRICE / VENDOR

RECOMMENDED BY

OCCASION / GIFT FOR

WINE NAME

VINTAGE SPECIFICS

PRICE / VENDOR

RECOMMENDED BY

OCCASION / GIFT FOR

 *ine was created from the beginning to make men joyful, and not to make them drunk.*

ECCLESIASTICUS 5:35, *THE APOCRYPHA*

DATE	LOCATION	WINE TO BE SOLD

DATE	LOCATION	WINE TO BE SOLD

f a man deliberately abstains from wine to such an extent that he does serious harm to his nature, he will not be free from blame.

SAINT THOMAS AQUINAS

55

WINE NAME

SPECIFICS / DESCRIPTION

PRICE / VENDOR

DATE PURCHASED

DATE STORED

STORAGE DETAILS

DRINK-BY DATE

WINE NAME

SPECIFICS / DESCRIPTION

PRICE / VENDOR

DATE PURCHASED

DATE STORED

STORAGE DETAILS

DRINK-BY DATE

*an in no one respect resembles wine;
For man by age is made intolerable,
But age improves all wine.*

ALEXIS, GREEK DRAMATIST (4TH CENTURY BC)

WINE NAME

SPECIFICS / DESCRIPTION

PRICE / VENDOR

DATE PURCHASED

DATE STORED

STORAGE DETAILS

DRINK-BY DATE

WINE NAME

SPECIFICS / DESCRIPTION

PRICE / VENDOR

DATE PURCHASED

DATE STORED

STORAGE DETAILS

DRINK-BY DATE

WINE NAME

SPECIFICS / DESCRIPTION

PRICE / VENDOR

DATE PURCHASED

DATE STORED

STORAGE DETAILS

DRINK-BY DATE

WINE NAME

SPECIFICS / DESCRIPTION

PRICE / VENDOR

DATE PURCHASED

DATE STORED

STORAGE DETAILS

DRINK-BY DATE

WINE NAME

SPECIFICS / DESCRIPTION

PRICE / VENDOR

DATE PURCHASED

DATE STORED

STORAGE DETAILS

DRINK-BY DATE

WINE NAME

SPECIFICS / DESCRIPTION

PRICE / VENDOR

DATE PURCHASED

DATE STORED

STORAGE DETAILS

DRINK-BY DATE

WINE NAME

SPECIFICS / DESCRIPTION

PRICE / VENDOR

DATE PURCHASED

DATE STORED

STORAGE DETAILS

DRINK-BY DATE

WINE NAME

SPECIFICS / DESCRIPTION

PRICE / VENDOR

DATE PURCHASED

DATE STORED

STORAGE DETAILS

DRINK-BY DATE

WINE NAME

SPECIFICS / DESCRIPTION

PRICE / VENDOR

DATE PURCHASED

DATE STORED

STORAGE DETAILS

DRINK-BY DATE

WINE NAME

SPECIFICS / DESCRIPTION

PRICE / VENDOR

DATE PURCHASED

DATE STORED

STORAGE DETAILS

DRINK-BY DATE

WINE NAME

SPECIFICS / DESCRIPTION

PRICE / VENDOR

DATE PURCHASED

DATE STORED

STORAGE DETAILS

DRINK-BY DATE

WINE NAME

SPECIFICS / DESCRIPTION

PRICE / VENDOR

DATE PURCHASED

DATE STORED

STORAGE DETAILS

DRINK-BY DATE

WINE NAME

SPECIFICS / DESCRIPTION

PRICE / VENDOR

DATE PURCHASED

DATE STORED

STORAGE DETAILS

DRINK-BY DATE

WINE NAME

SPECIFICS / DESCRIPTION

PRICE / VENDOR

DATE PURCHASED

DATE STORED

STORAGE DETAILS

DRINK-BY DATE

WINE NAME

SPECIFICS / DESCRIPTION

PRICE / VENDOR

DATE PURCHASED

DATE STORED

STORAGE DETAILS

DRINK-BY DATE

he very best of vineyards is the cellar.

LORD BYRON

61

WINE NAME

SPECIFICS / DESCRIPTION

PRICE / VENDOR

DATE PURCHASED

DATE STORED

STORAGE DETAILS

DRINK-BY DATE

WINE NAME

SPECIFICS / DESCRIPTION

PRICE / VENDOR

DATE PURCHASED

DATE STORED

STORAGE DETAILS

DRINK-BY DATE

WINE NAME

SPECIFICS / DESCRIPTION

PRICE / VENDOR

DATE PURCHASED

DATE STORED

STORAGE DETAILS

DRINK-BY DATE

WINE NAME

SPECIFICS / DESCRIPTION

PRICE / VENDOR

DATE PURCHASED

DATE STORED

STORAGE DETAILS

DRINK-BY DATE

WINE NAME

SPECIFICS / DESCRIPTION

PRICE / VENDOR

DATE PURCHASED

DATE STORED

STORAGE DETAILS

DRINK-BY DATE

 *house with a great wine stored below lives in our imagination as a joyful house, fast and splendidly rooted in the soil.*

GEORGE MEREDITH

WINE NAME

SPECIFICS / DESCRIPTION

PRICE / VENDOR

DATE PURCHASED

DATE STORED

STORAGE DETAILS

DRINK-BY DATE

WINE NAME

SPECIFICS / DESCRIPTION

PRICE / VENDOR

DATE PURCHASED

DATE STORED

STORAGE DETAILS

DRINK-BY DATE

WINE NAME

SPECIFICS / DESCRIPTION

PRICE / VENDOR

DATE PURCHASED

DATE STORED

STORAGE DETAILS

DRINK-BY DATE

WINE NAME

SPECIFICS / DESCRIPTION

PRICE / VENDOR

DATE PURCHASED

DATE STORED

STORAGE DETAILS

DRINK-BY DATE

WINE NAME

SPECIFICS / DESCRIPTION

PRICE / VENDOR

DATE PURCHASED

DATE STORED

STORAGE DETAILS

DRINK-BY DATE

WINE NAME

SPECIFICS / DESCRIPTION

PRICE / VENDOR

DATE PURCHASED

DATE STORED

STORAGE DETAILS

DRINK-BY DATE

WINE NAME

SPECIFICS / DESCRIPTION

PRICE / VENDOR

DATE PURCHASED

DATE STORED

STORAGE DETAILS

DRINK-BY DATE

WINE NAME

SPECIFICS / DESCRIPTION

PRICE / VENDOR

DATE PURCHASED

DATE STORED

STORAGE DETAILS

DRINK-BY DATE

*od in his goodness sent the grapes
to cheer both great and small;
little fools will drink too much
and great fools none at all.*

ANONYMOUS

WINE NAME

SPECIFICS / DESCRIPTION

PRICE / VENDOR

DATE PURCHASED

DATE STORED

STORAGE DETAILS

DRINK-BY DATE

WINE NAME

SPECIFICS / DESCRIPTION

PRICE / VENDOR

DATE PURCHASED

DATE STORED

STORAGE DETAILS

DRINK-BY DATE

WINE NAME

SPECIFICS / DESCRIPTION

PRICE / VENDOR

DATE PURCHASED

DATE STORED

STORAGE DETAILS

DRINK-BY DATE

On a moonlit night, after a snowfall, or under cherry blossoms, it adds to our pleasure if, while chatting at our ease, we bring forth the wine cups. Liquor is cheering on days when we are bored, or when a friend pays an unexpected visit. It is exceedingly agreeable too when you are offered cakes and wine most elegantly from behind a screen of state by a person of quality you do not know especially well. In winter it is delightful to sit opposite an intimate friend in a small room, toasting something to eat over the fire, and to drink deeply together.

YOSHIDA KENKO: *ESSAYS IN IDLENESS*, JAPANESE
PHILOSOPHER (C.1282-1350)

WINING
and DINING

WINING AND DINING

WINE

MEAL

OCCASION

PRICE / VENDOR

DESCRIPTION

WINE

MEAL

OCCASION

PRICE / VENDOR

DESCRIPTION

WINE

MEAL

OCCASION

PRICE / VENDOR

DESCRIPTION

 *ood wine is a good familiar creature if it be well used.*

WILLIAM SHAKESPEARE: *OTHELLO*

WINE

MEAL

OCCASION

PRICE / VENDOR

DESCRIPTION

WINE

MEAL

OCCASION

PRICE / VENDOR

DESCRIPTION

WINE

MEAL

OCCASION

PRICE / VENDOR

DESCRIPTION

WINE

MEAL

OCCASION

PRICE / VENDOR

DESCRIPTION

WINING AND DINING

WINE

MEAL

OCCASION

PRICE / VENDOR

DESCRIPTION

WINE

MEAL

OCCASION

PRICE / VENDOR

DESCRIPTION

WINE

MEAL

OCCASION

PRICE / VENDOR

DESCRIPTION

WINE

MEAL

OCCASION

PRICE / VENDOR

DESCRIPTION

WINE

MEAL

OCCASION

PRICE / VENDOR

DESCRIPTION

WINE

MEAL

OCCASION

PRICE / VENDOR

DESCRIPTION

WINE

MEAL

OCCASION

PRICE / VENDOR

DESCRIPTION

WINE

MEAL

OCCASION

PRICE / VENDOR

DESCRIPTION

WINING AND DINING

WINE

MEAL

OCCASION

PRICE / VENDOR

DESCRIPTION

WINE

MEAL

OCCASION

PRICE / VENDOR

DESCRIPTION

WINE

MEAL

OCCASION

PRICE / VENDOR

DESCRIPTION

 have lived temperately, eating little animal food. Vegetables constitute my principal diet. I double, however, the doctor's glass and a half of wine, and even treble it with a friend.

THOMAS JEFFERSON

WINE

MEAL

OCCASION

PRICE / VENDOR

DESCRIPTION

WINE

MEAL

OCCASION

PRICE / VENDOR

DESCRIPTION

WINE

MEAL

OCCASION

PRICE / VENDOR

DESCRIPTION

WINE

MEAL

OCCASION

PRICE / VENDOR

DESCRIPTION

inetasting, in the classic phrase, is a diverting pastime for young and old, for ladies as well as men. It is not so intellectual as chamber music, it is not so light-hearted as strip-tease; no one will...entangle you with problems that need an intimate understanding of Einstein and a slide-rule to answer. It is, in fact, the ideal pursuit with which to while away those hours between eleven in the morning and four in the afternoon.

B.A. YOUNG, ENGLISH WRITER

WINE-
TASTING
CLUBS

MEMBER NAME	PHONE NUMBER

DATE   LOCATION

he art of tasting wine is the performance of a sacred rite, which deserves to be carried out with the most grave and serious attention.

FRENCH NATIONAL COMMITTEE FOR WINE PUBLICITY

WINE TASTED

DATE / LOCATION

RATING / REVIEW

WINE TASTED

DATE / LOCATION

RATING / REVIEW

WINE TASTED

DATE / LOCATION

RATING / REVIEW

WINE TASTED

DATE / LOCATION

RATING / REVIEW

ne not only drinks wine, one smells it, observes it, tastes it, sips it and – one talks about it.

KING EDWARD VII

WINE TASTED

DATE / LOCATION

RATING / REVIEW

WINE TASTED

DATE / LOCATION

RATING / REVIEW

WINE TASTED

DATE / LOCATION

RATING / REVIEW

WINE TASTED

DATE / LOCATION

RATING / REVIEW

WINE TASTED

DATE / LOCATION

RATING / REVIEW

WINE TASTED

DATE / LOCATION

RATING / REVIEW

WINE-TASTING CLUBS – WINE-TASTING RECORD

WINE TASTED

DATE / LOCATION

RATING / REVIEW

WINE TASTED

DATE / LOCATION

RATING / REVIEW

WINE TASTED

DATE / LOCATION

RATING / REVIEW

WINE TASTED

DATE / LOCATION

RATING / REVIEW

WINE TASTED

DATE / LOCATION

RATING / REVIEW

WINE TASTED

DATE / LOCATION

RATING / REVIEW

WINE TASTED

DATE / LOCATION

RATING / REVIEW

WINE TASTED

DATE / LOCATION

RATING / REVIEW

WINE TASTED

DATE / LOCATION

RATING / REVIEW

WINE TASTED

DATE / LOCATION

RATING / REVIEW

*his wine should be eaten,
it is too good to be drunk.*

JONATHAN SWIFT (1667-1745)

WINE-TASTING CLUBS – WINE-TASTING RECORD

WINE TASTED

DATE / LOCATION

RATING / REVIEW

WINE TASTED

DATE / LOCATION

RATING / REVIEW

WINE TASTED

DATE / LOCATION

RATING / REVIEW

WINE TASTED

DATE / LOCATION

RATING / REVIEW

WINE TASTED

DATE / LOCATION

RATING / REVIEW

WINE TASTED

DATE / LOCATION

RATING / REVIEW

WINE TASTED

DATE / LOCATION

RATING / REVIEW

WINE TASTED

DATE / LOCATION

RATING / REVIEW

WINE TASTED

DATE / LOCATION

RATING / REVIEW

WINE TASTED

DATE / LOCATION

RATING / REVIEW

 *t's a naive domestic Burgundy without any breeding, but I believe you'll be amused by its presumption.*

JAMES THURBER

WINE TASTED

DATE / LOCATION

RATING / REVIEW

WINE TASTED

DATE / LOCATION

RATING / REVIEW

WINE TASTED

DATE / LOCATION

RATING / REVIEW

WINE TASTED

DATE / LOCATION

RATING / REVIEW

ome quickly, I am tasting stars!

DOM PERIGNON: UPON FIRST TASTING CHAMPAGNE,
FRENCH BENEDICTINE MONK (1638-1715)

WINE TASTED

DATE / LOCATION

RATING / REVIEW

WINE TASTED

DATE / LOCATION

RATING / REVIEW

WINE TASTED

DATE / LOCATION

RATING / REVIEW

WINE TASTED

DATE / LOCATION

RATING / REVIEW

WINE TASTED

DATE / LOCATION

RATING / REVIEW

WINE TASTED

DATE / LOCATION

RATING / REVIEW

WINE TASTED

DATE / LOCATION

RATING / REVIEW

WINE TASTED

DATE / LOCATION

RATING / REVIEW

WINE TASTED

DATE / LOCATION

RATING / REVIEW

WINE TASTED

DATE / LOCATION

RATING / REVIEW

WINE TASTED

DATE / LOCATION

RATING / REVIEW

WINE TASTED

DATE / LOCATION

RATING / REVIEW

WINE TASTED

DATE / LOCATION

RATING / REVIEW

WINE TASTED

DATE / LOCATION

RATING / REVIEW

WINE TASTED

DATE / LOCATION

RATING / REVIEW

WINE TASTED

DATE / LOCATION

RATING / REVIEW

WINE TASTED

DATE / LOCATION

RATING / REVIEW

WINE TASTED

DATE / LOCATION

RATING / REVIEW

No wine, no company; no wine, no conversation.

CHINESE PROVERB

I drink champagne when I'm happy and when I'm sad. Sometimes I drink it when I'm alone. When I have company I consider it obligatory. I trifle with it when I'm not hungry and drink it when I am. Otherwise I never touch it – unless I'm thirsty.

LILY BOLLINGER: *LA GRANDE DAME DU CHAMPAGNE,*
FRENCH VINTNER (1899-1977)

DIVINE
WINES

DIVINE WINES – FAVORITE RED WINES BY REGION

REGION:

WINE NAME

REGION:

WINE NAME

92

REGION: _____

WINE NAME _____

_____
_____
_____
_____
_____
_____
_____
_____
_____
_____
_____
_____
_____

REGION: _____

WINE NAME _____

_____
_____
_____
_____
_____
_____
_____
_____
_____
_____
_____
_____
_____
_____
_____
_____
_____

he wines that one remembers best are not necessarily the finest that one has tasted, and the highest quality may fail to delight as some far more humble beverage drunk in more favorable surroundings.

H. WARNER ALLEN

REGION:

WINE NAME

REGION:

WINE NAME

YEAR:

WINE NAME

YEAR:

WINE NAME

VINTNER:

WINE NAME

VINTNER:

WINE NAME

*ed wine
for children,
champagne
for men,
and brandy
for soldiers.*

OTTO VON BISMARCK,
(1815-1898)

REGION:

WINE NAME

REGION:

WINE NAME

REGION:

WINE NAME

REGION:

WINE NAME

REGION: _____

WINE NAME _____

_____
_____
_____
_____
_____
_____
_____
_____
_____
_____
_____
_____
_____
_____
_____
_____
_____
_____

REGION: _____

WINE NAME _____

_____
_____
_____
_____
_____
_____
_____
_____
_____
_____
_____
_____
_____
_____
_____
_____
_____
_____
_____
_____

ine is the milk of the gods, milk the drink of babies, tea the drink of women, and water the drink of the beasts.

JOHN STUART BLACKIE, SCOTTISH SCHOLAR (1809-1895)

YEAR:

WINE NAME

YEAR:

WINE NAME

VINTNER:

WINE NAME

VINTNER:

WINE NAME

_____   _____
_____   _____
_____   _____
_____   _____
_____   _____
_____   _____
_____   _____
_____   _____
_____   _____
_____   _____
_____   _____
_____   _____
_____   _____
_____   _____
_____   _____
_____   _____
_____   _____
_____   _____
_____   _____
_____   _____
_____   _____
_____   _____
_____   _____

he best kind of wine is that which is most pleasant to him who drinks it.

PLINY THE ELDER: *NATURAL HISTORY*

What is this life you are so sure about? A flame that kindles, flashes, and goes out. The unchanging heaven and eternal sea serve but to mock our mutability. And you before this wine who hesitate – for what, I ask you frankly, do you wait?

LI PO, CHINESE POET (C.700-762)

THE FESTIVAL
OF WINE

FESTIVAL

DATE / LOCATION

NOTES

FESTIVAL

DATE / LOCATION

NOTES

FESTIVAL

DATE / LOCATION

NOTES

FESTIVAL

DATE / LOCATION

NOTES

FESTIVAL

DATE / LOCATION

NOTES

FESTIVAL

DATE / LOCATION

NOTES

FESTIVAL

DATE / LOCATION

NOTES

FESTIVAL

DATE / LOCATION

NOTES

FESTIVAL

DATE / LOCATION

NOTES

FESTIVAL

DATE / LOCATION

NOTES

 *drink eternally. This is to me an eternity of drinking and drinking of eternity.... I moisten my windpipe with wine – I drink to banish all fear of dying – drink but deep enough and you shall live forever.*

FRANCOIS RABELAIS: *LIFE OF GARGANTUA AND PANTAGRUEL*, FRENCH AUTHOR, MONK AND DOCTOR (C.1494-1553)

TOUR COMPANY

LOCATION / PHONE NUMBER

NOTES

TOUR COMPANY

LOCATION / PHONE NUMBER

NOTES

TOUR COMPANY

LOCATION / PHONE NUMBER

NOTES

TOUR COMPANY

LOCATION / PHONE NUMBER

NOTES

*e that drinks is immortal
for wine still supplies
what age wears away;
how can he be dust
that moistens his clay?*

HENRY PURCELL, ENGLISH COMPOSER
(1659-1695)

TOUR COMPANY

LOCATION / PHONE NUMBER

NOTES

TOUR COMPANY

LOCATION / PHONE NUMBER

NOTES

TOUR COMPANY

LOCATION / PHONE NUMBER

NOTES

TOUR COMPANY

LOCATION / PHONE NUMBER

NOTES

TOUR COMPANY

LOCATION / PHONE NUMBER

NOTES

TOUR COMPANY

LOCATION / PHONE NUMBER

NOTES

WINERY

LOCATION / PHONE NUMBER

WINE SPECIALITIES

NOTES

WINERY

LOCATION / PHONE NUMBER

WINE SPECIALITIES

NOTES

WINERY

LOCATION / PHONE NUMBER

WINE SPECIALITIES

NOTES

WINERY

LOCATION / PHONE NUMBER

WINE SPECIALITIES

NOTES

WINERY

LOCATION / PHONE NUMBER

WINE SPECIALITIES

NOTES

WINERY

LOCATION / PHONE NUMBER

WINE SPECIALITIES

NOTES

WINERY

LOCATION / PHONE NUMBER

WINE SPECIALITIES

NOTES

WINERY

LOCATION / PHONE NUMBER

WINE SPECIALITIES

NOTES

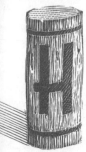

*e remains a fool his whole life long
who loves not women, wine and song.*

MARTIN LUTHER

THE FESTIVAL OF WINE – WINERIES

WINERY

LOCATION / PHONE NUMBER

WINE SPECIALITIES

NOTES

WINERY

LOCATION / PHONE NUMBER

WINE SPECIALITIES

NOTES

WINERY

LOCATION / PHONE NUMBER

WINE SPECIALITIES

NOTES

WINERY

LOCATION / PHONE NUMBER

WINE SPECIALITIES

NOTES

WINERY

LOCATION / PHONE NUMBER

WINE SPECIALITIES

NOTES

WINERY

LOCATION / PHONE NUMBER

WINE SPECIALITIES

NOTES

WINERY

LOCATION / PHONE NUMBER

WINE SPECIALITIES

NOTES

WINERY

LOCATION / PHONE NUMBER

WINE SPECIALITIES

NOTES

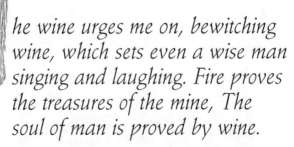

he wine urges me on, bewitching wine, which sets even a wise man singing and laughing. Fire proves the treasures of the mine, The soul of man is proved by wine.

THEOGNIS, GREEK POET (6TH CENTURY BC)

113

WINERY

LOCATION / PHONE NUMBER

WINE SPECIALITIES

NOTES

WINERY

LOCATION / PHONE NUMBER

WINE SPECIALITIES

NOTES

WINERY

LOCATION / PHONE NUMBER

WINE SPECIALITIES

NOTES

WINERY

LOCATION / PHONE NUMBER

WINE SPECIALITIES

NOTES

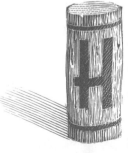 *e that is penniless is rich, and even the wealthy find their hearts expanding when they are smitten by the arrows of the vine.*

PINDAR: *EULOGIES*

WINERY

LOCATION / PHONE NUMBER

WINE SPECIALITIES

NOTES

WINERY

LOCATION / PHONE NUMBER

WINE SPECIALITIES

NOTES

WINERY

LOCATION / PHONE NUMBER

WINE SPECIALITIES

NOTES

WINERY

LOCATION / PHONE NUMBER

WINE SPECIALITIES

NOTES

WINERY

LOCATION / PHONE NUMBER

WINE SPECIALITIES

NOTES

WINERY

LOCATION / PHONE NUMBER

WINE SPECIALITIES

NOTES

WINERY

LOCATION / PHONE NUMBER

WINE SPECIALITIES

NOTES

WINERY

LOCATION / PHONE NUMBER

WINE SPECIALITIES

NOTES

WINERY

LOCATION / PHONE NUMBER

WINE SPECIALITIES

NOTES

WINERY

LOCATION / PHONE NUMBER

WINE SPECIALITIES

NOTES

WINERY

LOCATION / PHONE NUMBER

WINE SPECIALITIES

NOTES

WINERY

LOCATION / PHONE NUMBER

WINE SPECIALITIES

NOTES

WINERY

LOCATION / PHONE NUMBER

WINE SPECIALITIES

NOTES

WINERY

LOCATION / PHONE NUMBER

WINE SPECIALITIES

NOTES

ill ev'ry glass, for wine inspires us, and fires us with courage, love and joy.

JOHN GAY: *THE BEGGAR'S OPERA* (1728)

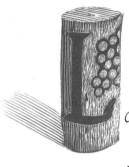

ove and wine are the bonds
that fasten us all,

The world but for these to
confusion would fall,

Were it not for the pleasures
of love and good wine,

Mankind, for each trifle their
lives would resign;

They'd not value dull life nor
could live without thinking,

Nor would kings rule the world
but for love and good drinking.

TOAST OF 1675

ALL ABOUT
WINE

ALL ABOUT WINE – BOOKS ABOUT WINE

TITLE

AUTHOR

NOTES

TITLE

AUTHOR

NOTES

TITLE

AUTHOR

NOTES

TITLE

AUTHOR

NOTES

TITLE

AUTHOR

NOTES

TITLE

AUTHOR

NOTES

TITLE

AUTHOR

NOTES

TITLE

AUTHOR

NOTES

TITLE

AUTHOR

NOTES

TITLE

AUTHOR

NOTES

here there is no wine, love perishes, and everything else that is pleasant to man. EURIPIDES: *THE BACCHAE*

TITLE

SUBSCRIPTION INFO

NOTES

TITLE

SUBSCRIPTION INFO

NOTES

TITLE

SUBSCRIPTION INFO

NOTES

TITLE

SUBSCRIPTION INFO

NOTES

TITLE

SUBSCRIPTION INFO

NOTES

TITLE

SUBSCRIPTION INFO

NOTES

TITLE

SUBSCRIPTION INFO

NOTES

TITLE

SUBSCRIPTION INFO

NOTES

TITLE

SUBSCRIPTION INFO

NOTES

TITLE

SUBSCRIPTION INFO

NOTES

TITLE

SUBSCRIPTION INFO

NOTES

TITLE

SUBSCRIPTION INFO

NOTES

TITLE

SUBSCRIPTION INFO

NOTES

TITLE

SUBSCRIPTION INFO

NOTES

TITLE

SUBSCRIPTION INFO

NOTES

pon the first goblet he read this inscription, monkey wine; *upon the second,* lion wine; *upon the third,* sheep wine; *upon the fourth,* swine wine. *These four inscriptions expressed the four descending degrees of drunkenness: the first, that which enlivens; the second, that which irritates; the third, that which stupefies; finally the last, that which brutalizes.*

VICTOR HUGO: *LES MISÉRABLES* (1862)

TITLE

SUBSCRIPTION INFO

NOTES

TITLE

SUBSCRIPTION INFO

NOTES

TITLE

SUBSCRIPTION INFO

NOTES

TITLE

SUBSCRIPTION INFO

NOTES

TITLE

SUBSCRIPTION INFO

NOTES

TITLE

SUBSCRIPTION INFO

NOTES

TITLE

WEB ADDRESS

NOTES

TITLE

WEB ADDRESS

NOTES

TITLE

WEB ADDRESS

NOTES

TITLE

WEB ADDRESS

NOTES

TITLE

WEB ADDRESS

NOTES

TITLE

WEB ADDRESS

NOTES

TITLE

WEB ADDRESS

NOTES

TITLE

WEB ADDRESS

NOTES

TITLE

WEB ADDRESS

NOTES

TITLE

WEB ADDRESS

NOTES

*ine prepares the heart for love,
Unless you take too much.*

OVID, *THE ART OF LOVE*

*hat contemptible scoundrel
stole the cork from my lunch?*

W.C. FIELDS (1880-1946)

ine, it's in my veins and I can't get it out.

BURGESS MEREDITH

lthough man is already ninety per cent water, the Prohibitionists are not yet satisfied.

JOHN KENDRICK BANGS, AMERICAN HUMORIST (1862-1922)

There are two reasons for drinking wine. When you are thirsty, to cure it; the other, when you are not thirsty, to prevent it. Prevention is better than cure.

THOMAS LOVE PEACOCK: *MELINCOUR*

WINE for the NEOPHYTE OENOPHILE

Buying Wine

Yes, it is important to buy from a reputable wine agent, merchant, or winery. The quality of wine will be determined in part by the type of seller and the conditions under which the wine is stored. For instance, wine you buy at the grocery store will only be a serviceable wine. The truly discerning buy wine as close to the source as possible, thus avoiding possible faults in storage.

IS PRICE A GOOD INDICATOR OF QUALITY?

Yes and no. There are always excellent vintages which, while inexpensive, have not yet been "discovered." If you discover one of these tell only your very best friends because soon your secret bargain will become everyone's expensive table wine. Like many other consumer products, wine's price generally reflects its care and/or perceived value. This is not always true. Some years ago, a bottle of wine from the cellar of Benjamin Franklin fetched $100,000 at auction and all wine experts agreed that the wine inside the bottle was worthless and should not be consumed. This is an extreme example because of the historical significance of the wine, but it does illustrate that price is not always a guarantee of an exceptional wine.

ine in itself is an excellent thing. POPE PIUS XII

Grape Varieties

There are an estimated 8000 grape varieties currently identified. The six most common varieties – cabernet sauvignon, pinot noir, merlot, chardonnay, sauvignon blanc, riesling – are the most popular because they are the most accessible to the neophyte palate. Explore the vast array of other varietals as part of your "vinification." In this age of genetic manipulation, new varieties are emerging all the time. For a comprehensive listing, consult one of the many excellent books about wine available at your local bookstore or library.

WHY IS ONE YEAR (or VINTAGE) CONSIDERED BETTER THAN ANOTHER? HOW DO YOU KNOW WHICH YEAR IS BEST?

The factors that influence the quality of a particular vintage are, in no particular order: temperature, humidity, rainfall, and hours of sunlight. The combination of these factors can affect vintages from year to year. For instance, one year's cabernet franc may be inferior, while better conditions can make the following year's vintage a prize-winning keeper.

The only way to know which vintage is best is by doing your homework. Read wine columns in newspapers, subscribe to wine newsletters, join a wine-tasting club, visit wine web sites, read books about wine, visit wineries, and consult the experts at your local wine merchant.

Deciphering the Wine Label

The wine label should contain all the information you need to know about the wine inside the bottle. In North America, regulations have been established to clarify the labels on imported wine. The label should tell you a number of things about the wine, including:

1. The country of origin

2. The variety of wine (see Grape Varieties)

3. The appellation or geographic region
   (eg. Bordeaux, Rhine, Rioja)

4. The vintage or year the grapes were harvested

5. Whether the wine was made according to a
   varietal style (focusing on the characteristics
   of an individual grape), or has been blended.

6. The name of the agent or importer. This can
   be useful if you are particularly fond of a
   certain wine and wish to know more about
   the vineyard or the region.

7. The alcohol content

8. The volume of the bottle

9. The sulfite content (only some wineries),
   and whether it's organic

10. Some imported wines with no pretense towards
    true greatness will identify themselves as a
    "table wine" or "vin de pays."

Alsace

Bordeaux   *Burgundy*

Wine Bottles

The three most common wine bottle shapes – Bordeaux, Burgundy, German – emerged because different wine types keep better in different bottle shapes. These are not necessarily fast and firm rules, and as new estate wineries emerge, they may be bottling their wines in whatever bottle is most economical and readily available and/or most distinctive.

WINE LIS

At a Restaurant

If you don't see anything familiar and you don't feel adventurous, ask your waiter to recommend a wine. Some gourmets are concerned with matching wines with food and will tell you that it's critical to choose the "right" wine. If you are more of the gourmand variety, feel free to drink whatever wine you wish, with whatever dish. As a general rule, however, matching wine and food of similar richness and strength brings out the best in both. You'll find books filled with wine/meal recommendations in your library or bookstore.

Experience suggests that the price of wines in restaurants is generally twice the store price. This can make for very expensive bottles of wine. As a rule, the higher the cost of a restaurant's bottle of wine, the finer the quality. Presumably, if they have an extensive wine list, someone has exercised an expert opinion in their selection. Don't always turn up your nose at the house wines. There are some excellent modestly priced wines available by the glass, half-liter, and liter.

When the wine is brought to the table, the waiter generally presents the bottle to the person who ordered it for identification as the chosen wine. A knowledgeable server then offers the cork for inspection. It is not necessary to smell the cork, but it is advisable to look at it closely. A wet cork proves the bottle was stored correctly, that is, on its side. If the wine has been in constant contact with the cork, the cork will have swollen and kept air from seeping in. It is the presence of oxygen that causes wine to deteriorate. Bad bottles should be sent back for replacement.

Some acidic white wines will develop harmless tartrate crystals on the cork. Often referred to as "wine diamonds," they are crystallized tartaric acid, a major organic wine acid that creates the acidic and sharp taste in some wines. Tartaric acid may also create a flaky sediment in the wine which should not be considered an indication of bad wine. Some experts believe that the presence of tartaric crystals is a barometer of a superior white wine.

Drinking Wine

OPENING AND SERVING WINES

The colder the serving temperature, the more muted the wine's characteristics. A very cold wine hides many imperfections. For unpretentious white wines, sweet wines, and sparkling wines, experts recommend a temperature of 10° Celsius (50° Fahrenheit). For tonier whites, light reds, and rosés, a moderate chill – 16° Celsius (60° Fahrenheit) – will allow the characteristics of the wine to be more clearly identified. Generally, reds should be served at room temperature – 20° Celsius (68° Fahrenheit).

WINE GLASSES

It's fun to discover the variety of glasses – almost as much fun as collecting the wines to serve within them! Shown here are the standard glass shapes, but there are variations such as hock glasses, sherry copitas, and brandy snifters. Generally, the rim of the

ISO wine-tasting glass

Classic White

wine glass should curve in slightly to capture the wine's aroma and allow swirling which further releases the aroma. Champagne should be served in flutes rather than the saucer-style glasses, since a smaller surface area means fewer bubbles escape, and the champagne stays bubbly longer.

WINE TASTING

In his book *Travels with My Corkscrew*, wine expert Tony Aspler described an Alsatian Gewurztraminer as "a lumberjack wearing too much aftershave." Much fun can be made of the odd way in which wine can be described. Who but the wine expert could taste a wine and detect "bricks" or the slightest "mousiness"?

It is difficult for the novice to conceive of such "un-winelike" flavors. Having conducted hundreds of wine tastings, Mr. Aspler knows "this is the most daunting aspect of wine appreciation for the neophyte – how to find the words to describe a smell. And even before that, how to

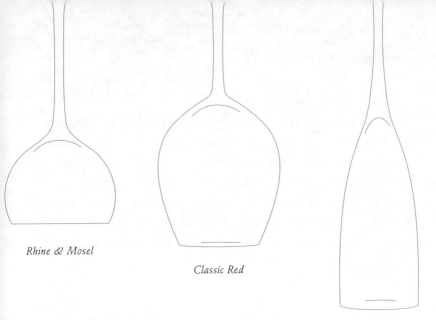

Rhine & Mosel

Classic Red

Champagne Flute

break down a bouquet into its component parts of oak, fruit character, and the organic smells that happen when wine is aged. You really can detect such smells as truffles, leather, coffee beans, bitter chocolate, seaweed, and iodine in the older reds. It just takes practice. The nose is like a muscle; the more you use it the more developed and acute it becomes." (from *Travels with My Corkscrew: Memoirs of a Wine Writer* by Tony Aspler. Toronto: McGraw-Hill Ryerson, 1997)

Here are some adjectives professional wine tasters use to describe the taste of wine: baked, barnyard, berrylike, big, bitter, bright, bricks, buttery, clean, cloying, coarse, crisp, delicate, dry, dusty, earthy, firm, flabby, flat, fleshy, flinty, foxy, mellow, moldy, mousy, oaky, salty, spicy, sulphury, sweet, tart, vinegary, watery, weighty, woody, yeasty.

Keeping Wine

STORING OPEN WINE

Ideally, one should never leave a bottle of wine half-full (or half-empty). Exposing wine to air causes the wine to deteriorate. If it cannot be avoided, however, extract as much oxygen as possible from the bottle with a wine pump or vacuum, and then seal it. There are also canister products on the market that replace the air with inert gases to prevent oxidization. While either method should prolong the characteristics of the wine, it is best to enjoy a wine when first opened. Drink up!

CELLARING WINE

Before you begin to stock your wine cellar, seriously consider your commitment to and enthusiasm for this endeavor. The investment of time and money required to create even a modestly comprehensive cellar should not be underestimated. There are few greater disappointments than opening a long-anticipated special bottle only to discover that it tastes "off" because it was improperly stored.

Basic Rules for Cellaring Wine
1. Store the wine on its side – the wine must always be in contact with the cork.

2. Keep the humidity high so the corks will stay moist and swollen.

3. Maintain a constant temperature. The ideal temperature is 13° Celsius (56° Fahrenheit). At 26° Celsius (75° Fahrenheit), wine will oxidize and go off.

4. Lower the lights. Bright lights can also cause oxidization.

5. Keep your wine far from strong odors and vibrating machines, like washers, power tools, and furnaces.